Unmasking The Candidate

I am appreciative to everyone that encouraged the writing of this book. To my buddy, an incredible person who spent countless hours listening and reading, I express my deepest gratitude and admiration.

You all know who you are.

Thank you!

Silence Facton

"Do-Good"

CONTENTS

Introduction

The biggest challenge I faced while investigating the facts, connecting dots and drafting this book was to maintain an open mind. I discovered lies I thought were truth. I uncovered disappointing events that unraveled my perception of Democracy and how We The People are governed and fed information.

The journey to uncovering deceit prior to the 2024 Presidential election begins with understanding what manipulation is, how it shows up, and what to do after learning you, we, me, have been bamboozled.

Manipulation implies the act of influencing or controlling someone or something in a skillful but often unfair or deceptive way. In the context of media and political activism, manipulation suggests the deliberate and strategic shaping or influencing of public opinion, political discourse, or behavior by selectively curating, framing, or distorting information.

Media outlets or activists emphasizing certain aspects of an issue or event while downplaying or ignoring important key facts influence opinions and decisions. By framing the information in a particular way, they steer their audience toward a preferred interpretation or conclusion that aligns with their agenda.

Agenda setting is a strategy highlighting specific topics or issues to make them more noticeable, or less, in public debates. By repeatedly focusing on certain subjects, media and activists guide the public's attention and influence which issues become central to political discussions and policymaking.

Manipulation may manifest through biased reporting or the presentation of information out of context. This can involve exaggeration, omission of key facts, or even the use of emotionally charged language to elicit strong responses, thereby swaying opinions by obscuring the full picture.

There are consequences for manipulating facts with misleading stories to influence the electorate. The intention of this book is to be an interruption in our rush to judgement about what we think is true. Hurt feelings and all. Tearing the bandage off is a short-lived pain. It has been written - "Truth will set us Free."

The consequences of agenda-driven storytelling and activism in media are most unfortunate for We The People. When truth to power is most needed, reliable journalism and media are hindered by lost credibility. How and when the media began a spiral to untrustworthy is revealed in the following pages.

The sucking sound of people being drawn into media manipulation and dividing society started spinning out-of-control in 1996-1999. Some readers just gasped, knowing what happened in the White House. Some people remain unaware and some readers, not yet born, need to know when lying was made acceptable in the USA from the Halls of Congress.

Living in a Post-Truth era where misleading stories supersede fact presents the need for me to verify and see for myself. The sanctimonious living among-us spew their commentary with certainty, disguising factual issues with distractive self-serving tales.

This book could be titled The Onion Story. Each layer revealed a trail of activism and actions leading straight to the 2024 Presidential election and how close we came to a Constitutional Crisis and the cliff's edge of the Republic's demise.

Silence Facton is a pseudonym to keep the focus on the events that happened, not the author. The facts speak for themselves. As the tendency for lying was rising and the standards for truth telling were falling in the 1990s, I put a note on the wall exiting our kitchen.

"how can you trust a liar, even when they are telling the truth?"

Anticipating some people reading this book will take offense to truths and consequences revealed, I suggest some people play a win-lose game. A win-win approach to problem solving that fosters collaboration and cooperation is ideal and progressive.

Celebrating or contributing to the demise of any political party is beyond the intent of this non-fiction book. The Republic needs multiple strong political parties competing fairly to check the balance of power.

For easy access to source material, scan the QR Code, or go to factonpublishing.com. Links to evidence, proof and verification of information in this book are provided for other non-trusters, and inquisitive minds.

Unmasking The Candidate is an explanation of media manipulation and lost credibility. Pulling back the curtain to reveal the underlying dishonesty and manipulation, by activist media, biased journalists, politicians and loyal influencers affecting the 2024 Presidential election.

Recognizing it hurts to be wrong, a look into the Mirror of Truth is a reckoning for healing and moving forward.

So, lets rip off the bandage...

Unmasking The Candidate

THE DECISION

Truth be told, society in the DysUnited States of America, DUSA, in 2024, was divided, lacking common sense and declining rapidly at the downfall of Trust in Government, journalism and the media.

How did the Republic get so close to the consequences of a constitutional crisis?

Short answer: Back-room deal making, with a concentration of decision-making power in the hands of a few, supported by activist media and influencers. A heavy dose of blind authoritarian arrogance sustained the effort to maintain control of the Government of DUSA.

Authoritarian actions occur when decisions are concentrated in a small group making appointments without participation by the people. These actions represent centralized Party control over the Government, the economy and society.

Candidly, The Democrat Party in 2024, along with activism in media and journalism, fiddled with concealing the President's mental abilities and got caught. Democrats were held accountable by voters for blurring truth and appointing a candidate. They gambled with deception and ended up paying the price. Election lost, credibility squandered, dazed and confused, the party of the people left the people's voice out of the choice and suffered defeat.

Objective journalism fell short in its role as guardian of truth to power. Caught up in partisanship and masquerading as self-proclaimed experts alongside celebrity influencers, they failed to critically scrutinize the legitimacy of a Presidential candidate.

Did machine politics expose the Democrat Party's totalitarian approach in selecting a candidate without an open primary?

It all began when manipulators concealing President Joe Biden's declining mental acuity were exposed for all to see during the Presidential debate between Joe Biden and Donald Trump on June 27, 2024.

If he cannot debate, how can he lead the Nation, or win an election? Staff using a mechanical auto-pen to sign documents on behalf of the President raises numerous conspiracy theories and legal questions surrounding the legitimacy of executive orders, policies and pardons.

President Biden's debate performance was widely criticized, with commentators noting he frequently lost his train of thought and gave meandering answers, had a faltering appearance, spoke with a hoarse voice, and failed to recall statistics or coherently express his opinion on several occasions.

On July 21, 2024, President Biden announced his withdrawal from the presidential race. [Link to source #1 – Withdrawal of Joe Biden - can be accessed at factonpublishing.com]

Biden addressed his performance, telling supporters at a rally in Raleigh, N.C. "I don't walk as easily as I used to. I don't speak as smoothly as I used to. I don't debate as well as I used to. But I know what I do know, I know how to tell the truth!"
[Link to source #2 – Joe Biden debate performance - at factonpublishing.com]

The accuracy of President Biden's self-proclaimed truth telling ability gets revealed along with other Presidential lies as we continue down the path of discovery and connecting dots.

Obvious to the public that the President's cognitive abilities were deteriorating, Party elites made a late campaign decision; eliminate Joe Biden and conduct a virtual rollcall of delegates to appoint Vice President Kamala Harris as The Party nominee and candidate for the 2024 Presidential election.

> Associated Press reported: "Harris officially claimed the nomination following a five-day online voting process, receiving 4,563 delegate votes out of 4,615 cast, or about 99% of participating delegates. A total of 52 delegates in 18 states cast their votes for "present," the only other option on the ballot." [source #3 – Harris nomination]

Nancy Pelosi, Speaker of The House of Representatives, the senior Democrat Party leader, spoke about the Harris loss and the lack of a Democrat Party open primary:

ABC News reported, Former Speaker of the House of Representatives, Nancy Pelosi, worked behind the scenes to urge Biden to drop out of the presidential race following his performance at the debate.

In portions of a New York Times podcast interview, as reported by ABC news, Speaker Pelosi blamed Vice President Kamala Harris' election loss on President Joe Biden's late exit from the presidential race and the lack of a Democrat primary.

> "The anticipation was that, if the president were to step aside, that there would be an open primary," Pelosi said. "And as I say, Kamala may have, I think

she would have done well in that and been stronger going forward. But we don't know that. That didn't happen. We live with what happened".

[source #4 – Pelosi blames Harris loss on Joe Biden]

Think about this...: if citizens are not included in the voting process during an open primary for President of the United States, can the candidate truly be considered legitimate?

If States have laws mandating primaries for General Election offices, President and Vice President, and a primary was not held, was State law violated? Do Party rules supersede State laws?

Would Electoral College votes count from States not holding mandatory primary elections?

If the voice of the People is subverted by The Party, does this violate the Fourteenth Amendment's Due Process clause?

If an illegitimate candidate wins a Presidential election, how would the Supreme Court and the populace reconcile the challenge of legitimacy?

Does the country go into a constitutional crisis? Does the Republic die at the hands of manipulators causing dysfunction?

Does civil war break-out in the Republic if an illegitimate candidate wins a Presidential election?

THE CANDIDATE

The ending of Joe Biden's re-election campaign for President signaled a strategic shift in the 2024 election. Attempts to conceal President Biden's declining mental alertness from the people amounted to a manipulative smokescreen. Party elites and leaders forced President Biden out of the election race and replaced him with Kamala Harris as their candidate for President.

If Kamala Harris had won the Presidential election in 2024, would she have been a legitimate President?

A virtual primary among Party Delegates without citizens participating in the primary election does not align with Democratic principles and a Constitutional People's Republic.

Circumventing the voice of the people carries consequences. Primaries serve to evaluate a candidate's electability and appeal to voters. Without this process, unvetted candidates might not reflect the will of the people or ability to with-stand public scrutiny. Delegates selecting the 2024 Presidential candidate was perceived as a decision made behind closed doors.

Did the candidate, Kamala Harris, reflect the will of the People or the will of Party elitists?

The voice of the people is essential for maintaining the balance of power. Without the voice of the people there is no choice, and without choice, there is no democracy and no Republic.

A keystone refers to the central, critical element that holds a system together. In our Republic, the continuous and active expression of the people's voice through elections, representation and policy feedback is what sustains our Republic and keeps its structure intact and functioning.

By sidelining the voice of the people, our Republic risked becoming an empty shell, a system in name only. Susceptible to creeping authoritarianism, or dictatorship by the offending Party. The people's voice compels leaders to serve the interests of all citizens rather than catering solely to party politics.

Diversity of opinions is essential for sound decision-making, ensuring fairness and equity. Active participation in elections is crucial, as it allows our Constitutional People's Republic to adapt and evolve in line with changing societal values and needs.

When citizens feel that their voices are being ignored or manipulated, their trust in government and elected officials erodes. When people believe that their votes and opinions no longer matter, apathy and frustration worsen. Suppressing the voice of the people serves those in power by allowing totalitarian tendencies to flourish.

Democrat Party elites, devotees and activist media spinning fear of a threat to democracy, while ignoring the people's voice in the 2024 Presidential election sabotaged the principles of democracy and the fundamental precepts of fairness and set the stage for a constitutional crisis.

A CONSTITUTIONAL CRISIS

A constitutional crisis can occur when the Constitution lacks clear guidance to resolve a particular issue, potentially undermining the government's stability and legitimacy while creating widespread uncertainty among the populace.

Is appointing a feasible illegitimate candidate, while concealing the declining mental acuity of an incumbent President, a deliberate attempt to seize the White House, control the Government?

Manipulating an election by promoting a potential illegitimate candidate and concealing truth from the people echoes the warnings in George Orwell's book, 1984, where The Party distorts truth to maintain power and control. [source #5 - Orwell]

Could it be that the Democrat Party, which worried citizens of a constitutional crisis, threats to democracy, and a battle for the soul of America, is the very party that pushed the People's Republic to the brink?

Excluding the people's voice in a primary election for a presidential candidate undermines the core principles of democracy and our Republic. Dismissing citizen involvement, the Party betrayed the trust of the people.

George Washington, the First President of the United States, in his Farewell Address of 1796, strongly warned against the dangers of political factions and partisan divisions. He believed that political parties could undermine national unity and lead to despotism.

Despotism is a form of governance or power where a single individual or a small group wields absolute and often oppressive authority over others, typically without regard for the rule-of-law, individual freedoms, or cultural principles.

Excerpt from President Washington's farewell address:

> "The alternate domination of one faction over another, sharpened by the spirit of revenge, natural to party dissension, which in different ages and countries has perpetrated the most horrid enormities, is itself a frightful despotism."

Washington cautioned that partisan politics could lead to the erosion of public trust, encourage foreign influence, and distract from the country's collective interests.

President Washington's advice was to prioritize national unity over partisan loyalties:

> "It serves always to distract the public councils and enfeeble the public administration. It agitates the community with ill-founded jealousies and false alarms, kindles the animosity of one part against another, [and] foments occasionally riot and insurrection."

Washington urged Americans to focus on unity and the common good over partisan interests.

George Washington's Farewell Address is a foundational document in American history. You can access the text at these sources:

Library of Congress: Offers a digitized version of the original manuscript: [source #6 – George Washington's Farewell address]

U.S. Senate: Provides a PDF version of the address, reflecting its significance in legislative history: [source #7]

Founders Online: Hosted by the National Archives: [source #8]

The Party

Ignoring President Washington's advice, the 2024 Democrat Party fell prey to a superiority syndrome developed from its long-established power. Eighty years of governance, rulemaking and political dominance bred arrogance, blinding them to commitments to truth, trust, and ethics.

Today, we experience the consequences of the Democrat Party's policies and persistent control of the DUSA Government.

The Democrat Party held the majority in the U.S. House of Representatives for much of the period between 1945 and 1995.

> Democrats controlled the U.S. House of Representatives for all but four years from 1945 to 1995:
>
> Republicans held the majority from 1947 to 1949 and again from 1953 to 1955.

Democrat Party dominance in the U.S. House of Representatives, especially from 1955 to 1995, was one of the longest stretches of single-party control in U.S. Congressional history. It ended with the Republican Revolution in the 1994 midterm elections, when Republicans gained control for the first time in 40 years. [source #9 – Republican Revolution]

The Democrats' experiment with one-party dominance ultimately collapsed under its own totalitarian suppression of free speech inflicted to maintain power. By stifling a diversity of ideas on university campuses, in politics, in the media, and among citizens, they fractured society. Their attempt to reshape America into a Marxist-style governance failed, as the common-sense voice of the people proved more powerful than the self-righteous elite.

Lessons learned: collaboration and cooperation stemming from free speech and open debate are required for a healthy two-party political system to survive.

The United States government functions as a Constitutional People's Republic because citizens elect representatives to safeguard our collective interests. Article IV Section 4 of The U.S. Constitution guarantees each state a Republican Form of Government.

U.S. Constitution:

"The United States shall guarantee to every State in this Union a Republican Form of Government, and shall protect each of them against Invasion; and on Application of the Legislature, or of the Executive (when the Legislature cannot be convened) against domestic Violence." [source #10 - U.S. Constitution guarantee]

James Madison emphasized popular sovereignty among the distinctive characteristics of the Republican form of government: Excerpt from the *Federalist No. 39* defining a Republican Government:

..."a government which derives all its powers directly or indirectly from the great body of the people, and is administered by persons holding their offices. *"*
[source #11 - Government derives power]

The foundation of a Constitutional Republic is the sanctity of the people's voice. Representation adhering to the rule of law ensures the power resides with the people.

The word democracy does not appear in the United States Constitution. Although often labeled as a democracy, the United States is more accurately defined as a Constitutional Republic that incorporates democratic principles of fairness and the rule of law. The Republic utilizes mechanisms such as the Electoral College, population-based representation, and judicial review, all designed to prevent unchecked majority rule.

Democracy is both a governing principle and a cultural mindset that values popular sovereignty and majority rule. In contrast, a Republic is a structured system of government in which citizens elect representatives to govern under a constitution and established rule of law.

Preamble to the Constitution of The United States of America:

"We the People of the United States, in Order to form a more perfect Union, establish Justice, insure domestic Tranquility, provide for the common defence, promote the general Welfare, and secure the Blessings of Liberty to ourselves and our Posterity, do ordain and establish this Constitution for the United States of America." [source #12 – Preamble to the Constitution]

THE BIG BAMBOOZLE

The "laptop from hell" belonging to Robert Hunter Biden, son of President Joe Biden, exposed the hypocrisy and bias of loyalist media, journalists, Democrat supporters, celebrity influencers and 51 high ranking U.S intelligence officials.

Defending the indefensible, the media's disinformation campaign and nothing-to-see here strategy shielded the legitimacy of Hunter's laptop from the public. Sanctimoniously shouting they were right and everyone else was wrong.

Regardless of the excuses or distractions by faithful Democrats, the evidence was in; the FBI confirmed the laptop was Hunter Biden's during Hunter's criminal trial in Delaware. [source #13 - FBI confirms laptop]

Democrats, activist media and journalists dismissed The New York Post's breaking story on Hunter Biden's laptop abandoned at a computer repair shop as "Russian disinformation". [source #14 - New York Post story]

The laptop containing evidence of dirty deeds was authentic. [source #15 - laptop from hell]

Former, and now disgraced intelligence officials, Democrats in Congress and then-candidate Joe Biden himself, all denied the accuracy of reports on the contents of the so-called "laptop from hell" in October 2020. [source #16 – intelligence officials]

On January 20, 2025, President Donald J. Trump signed an Executive Order stripping security clearances from 51 former intelligence officials. Excerpt from the Executive Order:

> "In the closing weeks of the 2020 Presidential campaign, at least 51 former intelligence officials coordinated with the Biden campaign to issue a letter discrediting the reporting that President Joseph R. Biden's son had abandoned his laptop at a computer repair business. Signatories of the letter falsely suggested that the news story was part of a Russian disinformation campaign."

> "Effective immediately, the Director of National Intelligence, in consultation with the Director of the Central Intelligence Agency, shall revoke any current or active clearances held by the following individuals:" [source # 17 – holding former government officials accountable]

Was the Democrat Party story, that the laptop was everything but Hunter's a purposeful omission of facts? Claiming it was Russian disinformation, the media, politicians and government officials concealed the Hunter Biden laptop evidence from the people prior to the 2020 election. Election interference? Dereliction of duties and responsibilities? Criminal activity?

Ratings, revenue, viewers, clicks and personal pride at risk, independent journalists, legacy media, talk TV, celebrity and social media influencers abandoned their responsibilities as impartial gatekeepers of Truth to Power. Trust in journalism and media vanished. How do we trust manipulators of truth and facts? We don't, we avoid them, we dismiss them, we change the channel.

Bias exposed; credibility wrecked by self-righteous preaching; Democrat devotees and deceivers collapsed trust in The Party. Activism in journalism and media contributed to the erosion. Intended or unintended; either way, long-term impacts on society are yet to be experienced.

The Democrat Party plunged to a sudden stop at the bottom, in a basket of distrust. Pointing fingers of blame everywhere except at themselves and their pattern of failed accountability, lack of truthfulness and disenfranchising the electorate.

Along with unwavering partisans, The Democrat Party led society to the brink. On November 5, 2024, the people's voice roared, decisively electing Donald J. Trump as President.

Trump Tantrum Syndrome escalated while Democrats shouted and screamed in opposition to the people's choice for a transparent Government and accountability for taxpayer's dollars. The Trump Administration released details on expenditures by the Biden Administration in-spite-of activist attempts to keep the facts hidden from the public.

Democrat partisans failed to hold themselves accountable, duping their followers and the American people by concealing truth with deceitful manipulation of information. The fight for the "Soul of America" was a campaign strategy deployed by Democrat Party strategists to frighten citizens about threats to democracy. Spread by activist media, celebrity influencers and party faithful, the messaging misled the public.

Journalists, politicians, media know-it-alls and celebrity influencers defending the indefensible pulled the rug out from under Trust and Integrity in Government, journalism and the media - destabilizing the Republic.

THE BAMBOOZLERS

How do you feel when you learn you have been tricked or deceived?

Bamboozle (verb): To deceive, trick, or confuse someone, often through cleverness, misdirection, or manipulation. The term can imply playful trickery or more serious deception, depending on context.

People react in a range of ways when they realize they have been bamboozled. Shock, disbelief, anger, frustration, embarrassment, defensive rationalization, and distrust identify several emotions connected to being hoodwinked.

Culturally, the term bamboozle has a mix of lighthearted and serious tones. Used for magic tricks, pranks, even marketing. Bamboozle is also encountered in scams, politics, and historical deception.

What happens when journalists, news outlets, media and influencers deceive their audience? How do we make informed decisions when information presented is distorted? How do we have conversations with family and friends?

How many examples do we need to confirm bamboozling happened? One example is good for some people. Others need to see evidence of multiple instances, a pattern. Events are what they are, and actions have consequences.

Objective reporting of facts enables independent thinking and decision making, free from the stress of who's right and who is wrong. Where do you get your information on politics and governance of the day? Is it important to know?

How do you form opinions of what is going on in the Government of the DysUnited States of America, DUSA? How do we prepare for what's next? Conflict at the top rolls downhill.

In 2025, some cities, in what was the USA, harbor criminal migrants, other cities do not. Some States support males playing in girls' sports, most do not. These are two of several examples supporting the concept that the United States of America is not United - it is DysUnited. Fractured, devoid of truth telling, and accountability. DUSA!

Bamboozling by people and organizations responsible for unbiased truthful journalism and news reporting, during the first twenty-five years of the 21st Century, resulted in the fox in the hen-house, cleaning house.

Credibility sacrificed, ethics cast aside, and trustworthiness in journalism, media and government evaporated, life in 2025 DUSA is the bamboozler era. How do you trust a bamboozler? How do you, we, all of us, live in a Post-Truth era?

The following pages connect events revealing how the lack of accountability, combined with activism in journalism and unethical news reporting spiraled into 21st Century failures to hold truth to power and the bamboozling of We The People living in the Post-Truth era.

THE POST-TRUTH ERA

How and when did the tipping point happen?

Short answer: failed accountability in 1999.

A visible display of media manipulation began in 1996, when a relationship between a 23-year-old intern and the President of The United States was uncovered. The revelation launched the media into a frenzy that exposed bias and deceptive news reporting.

The Post-Truth era is rooted in the Senate trial of President William (Bill) Clinton for perjury and obstructing justice. Sly as he was, on the hook of justice, his truth-bending and gamesmanship exposed the unwillingness of Democrat Party loyalists, journalists and activist media to hold themselves and their leader accountable for lying. Lying under oath and, to the American people.

Failure to hold The President accountable for lying to the court after swearing under oath to tell the truth set an example that lying was acceptable for generations to follow – "If he can do it, I can do it" mentality spread like a persistent virus. Diminishing how society values truth and law.

Beyond politicians fabricating stories and distorting truth, to rally the base and win votes, lying under oath violates the highest standard of truth. Swearing to tell the truth, the whole truth and nothing but the truth, is a pledge of integrity and honor.

The perjury charges incurred by President Clinton were associated to his testimony in a deposition for a sexual harassment lawsuit filed by Paula Jones. During the deposition, Clinton denied having a sexual relationship with White House intern Monica Lewinsky.

Investigations, including those led by Independent Counsel Kenneth Starr, uncovered evidence to the contrary, leading to the accusation that Clinton had committed perjury and obstructed justice by attempting to conceal the nature of his relationship with Lewinsky.

These charges were central to the articles of impeachment brought against him by the House of Representatives in 1998. While the House approved two articles of impeachment, perjury and obstruction of justice, President Clinton was ultimately acquitted by the Senate. The charges did not receive the two-thirds majority vote required for conviction.

Embraced by society, lying as acceptable behavior invaded our daily lives. Today, we live in a Post-Truth era gone berserk.

Etched in the marble Halls of Congress, lying had officially become an acceptable standard. Consequences rolling downhill onto our children and following generations. Democrat Leaders, journalists and media personalities condoning the President's lying under oath is a key historical tipping point to living in today's distorted society. A corruption of traditional values and structures.

Media coverage during the Clinton-Lewinsky scandal was littered with excuses and distractions. The President of The United States lied while under oath to a court - Democrats made it okay. A breach of trust leading to the tipping point into the Post-Truth era.

The trial of President Bill Clinton in the U.S, Senate for the crimes of perjury and obstruction of justice in 1999 was cast aside by Democrats, loyalists and activist media as a sex scandal. A done-by-others strategy to deflect from the real issue - lying under oath.

Senators voting not to hold the President accountable for lying did not heed the warning by Henry Hyde in his closing remarks during the trial on January 16, 1999.

House Judiciary Committee Chairman Henry Hyde emphasized the gravity of the charges and the importance of upholding the rule of law. He argued that the case was not about private matters but about public acts of perjury and obstruction of justice by the President, which he believed constituted a betrayal of public trust.

Hyde stated, "The matter before you is a question of the willful, premeditated, deliberate corruption of the nation's system of justice through perjury and obstruction of justice."

He concluded by urging the Senate to rise above politics and partisanship, asserting that the trial was a test of whether "sacred honor" still had meaning in contemporary America.

Sources for Representative Henry Hyde's closing remarks:
[source #18 - Hyde closing remarks]

Senate Trial of President William Jefferson Clinton:
[source #19 – January 16, 1999]

Video of Henry Hyde's closing argument on C-SPAN:
[source #20]

The Senate voted not to hold the President accountable for lying under oath. Millions of American parents, children, students, teachers, influencers, media personalities, preachers and politicians embraced lying as an acceptable behavior in society. Liars conquered the headlines and activist media influencers were emboldened. Lack of accountability led us down the path into the Post-Truth era.

Before we continue down the path, a quick look back at Presidential lying.

Yes, Presidents have and continue to lie. Humans lie. We mimic. When Republican President Richard Nixon got caught, facing embarrassment, humiliation and disgrace, he did what was best for the country, he resigned.

After Republican President George H. W. Bush, reneged on his "Read My Lips" promise not to impose new taxes, then imposed new taxes, he was voted out of office after a single term.

The Clinton team of loyalist Democrats pushed on like it was okay to lie after the Senate voted no punishment. After the trial, President Clinton admitted to inappropriate relations with Lewinsky. The manipulation of truth became a standard and invisible in Democrat's Mirror of Integrity.

Republican President George W. Bush, continued the pattern of deceit, claiming weapons of mass destruction to justify war in Iraq. The narrative playing on fears of mass casualties and the end of civilization was not supported. The war did not reveal the weapons they claimed.

Democrat President Barack Obama, lied to the world when he drew a "red-line" with President Assad's use of chemical weapons on the Syrian people. Line crossed, no response. Idle threat perceived as empty rhetoric.

President Obama's quote "if you like your doctor, you can keep your doctor" was a dagger in the heart of the people's trust in government and politicians.

Then along came Joe Biden, fighting for the "Soul of America" by frightening people about the death of democracy.

President Biden's broken promise not to interfere in the judicial proceedings of his son, Hunter, was another tipping point, shattering Trust in Government and the President.

He said he would not, and he did. Activists made excuses for the President pardoning his son who admitted guilt. The President just changed his mind swirled as their narrative, further exposing Democrat's failure to comprehend hypocrisy and the consequences that broken promises by leaders set bad examples for all to see and mimic.

President Joe Biden did not just lie to the American people; he broke the backbone of Trust - Integrity.

It was not about the act, the pardon, or the inappropriate behavior of an adult man with an intern in the White House. It was about lying and not being held accountable by journalists responsible for speaking Truth to power.

Democrats failed to hold President Bill Clinton accountable for lying after swearing to tell the truth to a court in a judicial proceeding. Saying he did not, then admitting he did.

President Joe Biden told America he would not, and he did. A continuation of a pattern of political leaders setting bad examples of unacceptable behavior.

Surrendering objective reporting, activist media that bamboozled America tipped the scales.

Is there any wonder why We The People are wading in a cesspool of lies, deceit and manipulation of facts in the Post-Truth era?

CONSEQUENCES

Sabotaging their own commitment to democracy, the Democrat political machine, along with activist media and affiliates, led the Nation to a close encounter with a constitutional crisis and collapse of the People's Constitutional Republic.

The Democrat Party's presidential campaign for Kamala Harris was entangled in deception from the very beginning. While we cannot change the past, we continue to experience its repercussions. It is crucial to recognize the sequence of actions, concealed truths, and subsequent consequences in order to navigate around the political sphere and policies to enjoy life as freely as possible.

Beyond individuals involved in a web of dishonesty and manipulation, responsibility also rests with news organizations entrusted to unearth and confirm facts. Activist journalism and news reporting weakened media credibility, trustworthiness and integrity.

How does a political party and their media machine lacking trustworthiness get out of a dysfunctional death spiral?

Democrat politicians and devotees, dazed and confused, scratching their heads wondering how they ended up in a basket of distrust, must recognize concealing facts combined with failure to hold themselves accountable caused political animosity and turmoil in DUSA. Democrats' resistance to everything strategy to escape the spiral to irrelevance, did not connect with the people. Sore losers caught with their hand and arm in the proverbial cookie jar.

Acknowledging their contribution to the decline of accountability, Trust and Integrity in DUSA is a necessary first step toward rebuilding The Democrat Party. The collapse of Trust in Party leaders, journalists and loyalists makes the way forward a formidable task.

Separating from individuals and special interest groups clinging to disingenuous partyspeak is a worthy second step for cleansing and restructuring The Party. Will Democrat politicians and loyalists acknowledge that an activist media concealing facts and twisting truths, shattered people's Trust in Government?

Neutral journalism, the final line in defense of our Republic, collapsed under the weight of The Party they collectively made excuses to support. Sanctimonious know-it-alls living among us bending facts and twisting truth provoked hate and discontent across society. Hatred for Donald Trump and MAGA, the Make America Great Again slogan that turned into a political movement, discombobulated Democrats and blinded the objectivity of politicians, activist influencers, journalists and media personalities.

Independent journalists and influencers dismissing an objective look at their performance digs the hole even deeper. Faithful Democrats dismissed Hunter Biden's laptop as Russian disinformation. Hiding behind a letter signed by biased and now disgraced intelligence officials.

Loyalist media neglected to hold The Party accountable for concealing President Biden's deteriorating mental faculties. Ironically, it was his mental fitness and natural aging processes that ended-up initiating a series of detrimental decisions by Democrat elites influencing the election with their chosen candidate – intended or unintended.

The Party fumbled The Candidate decision. They held a delegate-only virtual primary, leaving the voting public out of the nomination process. Ouch!

Credibility eroded. Integrity abandoned. Damage done! Will the next Democrat Party candidate for President of DUSA embody the same spirit as yesteryear and legacy leaders? Will The Democrat Party continue to deploy a whatever it takes strategy to regain control and power? Will activist media continue to bamboozle the people to support "their" side? Questions to consider going forward.

Failing to uphold the principles of democracy and protect the People's Constitutional Republic had outcomes. The election of Donald J. Trump and a shift to a Republican Party representing the people.

Finding truth in the Post-Truth era is a daunting challenge faced by everyone. Truth gets distorted to support strategies and plots to win control. Facts in the 21st Century political sphere are discarded as collateral damage. How do we find and validate facts as true and accurate?

Media and independent journalists abandoned their objectivity and neutrality by choosing sides. Their failure to investigate the legitimacy of The Candidate and honestly report to the American people will linger in society for generations. If they concealed President Biden's cognitive abilities and hid facts about Hunter's laptop, what else did the activist media conceal and distort?

Was there validity to the "stop the steal" vote count of the 2020 Presidential election? The popular vote for the Presidential election of Joe Biden in 2020 exceeded 81 million votes for the only time in history. Surpassing all other Presidential election tallies by a wide margin.

2024	Donald Trump	77,303,569
2020	Joe Biden	81,286,454
2016	Donald Trump	62,985,153
2012	Barack Obama	65,918,507
2008	Barack Obama	69,499,428
	[source # 21]	

Truth fell like dominoes after the failure to hold the President of the United States accountable for lying under oath twenty-five years ago, in 1999. Today, in 2025, we live with the consequences of those actions and a continuation of media manipulation combined with an accelerated invasion of sanctimonious influencers.

Our Republic narrowly escaped death behind the veil of censorship, propaganda and groupthink. Media manipulation distorted the truth, undermining credibility and trapped the Democrat Party in a delusional spin-cycle of resistance and political stunts. Their actions cast the Party into a self-inflicted sideshow.

THE AWAKENING

An awakening can be a profound shift. A moment when layers of old beliefs peel away to reveal a clearer, more honest view of oneself and the world. A change in perception revealing a new clarity. Long-held assumptions, patterns, or behaviors begin to lose their grip.

The realization that activism in journalism and the media, combined with biased influencers and decisions by elitest politicians caused the outcome of the 2024 Presidential election – a hard pill to swallow for some Democrats. Bamboozling the public into believing their versions of misleading Truth resulted in defeat and a dormant Democrat Party.

Voters in 2024 awakened to the manipulation and removed the reins of power from the grasp of the Democrat Party. Handing the Republican Party the task of correcting wrongs and undoing misdeeds.

THE TRUTH - ACCORDING TO WHOM

The Ministry of Truth in George Orwell's book, *1984*, captures the essence of The Party's control over what is truth. He highlighted how individual perception and critical thinking were systematically manipulated and suppressed.

> *"The Party told you to reject the evidence of your eyes and ears. It was their final, most essential command."*

A powerful reminder of the importance of questioning authority and valuing objective journalism. [source #22 – George Orwell]

Who will nominate the next Democrat candidate for President of DUSA? The Party or The People?

Time will tell. 2028 is a short distance around the bend on the path to the next free and fair election.

On April 27, 2022, President Biden and the Democrat Party using the Department of Homeland Security, activated the **Disinformation Governance Board**, echoing Orwell's depiction of a Ministry of Truth designed to restrict free speech. [source #23]

Biased influencers have been part of humanity since the existence of two humans, each trying to convince the other to do, or try something. Party faithful, influencers, journalists and activist media concealing facts and twisting truth set a series of consequences in motion.

Like ripples from a pebble in a pond, media activism expanded to a point of irrelevance. Altering society in ways we might never have anticipated. Finding Truth in a Post-Truth cultural war is a disturbing reality. Was undermining the voice of the People in the 2024 Presidential election a boulder in the pond of the People's Republic?

Here are few examples of methods used in unbalanced news reporting and media spin in 21st Century DUSA:

Selective Reporting

Definition: This occurs when media outlets choose to report only certain stories or aspects of a story, while ignoring others. This can create a skewed perception of events.

Example: A news outlet might focus extensively on negative aspects of a political figure's actions while ignoring positive developments.

Framing

Definition: Framing involves presenting information in a way that influences how it is interpreted. This can be done using specific language, tone, or context.

Example: Describing a protest as a "riot" versus a "demonstration" can significantly affect public perception.

The following examples demonstrate how word choice and framing in news reporting can shape public perception and influence opinions.

Immigration:

Positive Framing: Describing individuals as "undocumented immigrants" emphasizes their lack of legal status but avoids criminal connotations.

Negative Framing: Referring to individuals as "illegal aliens" can invoke a sense of criminality and fear.

Healthcare:

Positive Framing: Calling it "universal healthcare" highlights the inclusivity and accessibility of the system.

Negative Framing: Describing it as "socialized medicine" can invoke fears of government control and inefficiency.

Environmental Policy:

Positive Framing: Describing policies as "climate action" emphasizes proactive efforts to combat climate change.

Negative Framing: Referring to the same policies as "costly mandates" focuses on potential economic drawbacks.

Law Enforcement:

Positive Framing: Referring to actions as "community policing" suggests a collaborative and supportive approach.

Negative Framing: Calling it "aggressive policing" highlights potential confrontations and excessive force.

Economic Policy:

Positive Framing: Describing tax cuts as "tax relief" frames them as beneficial and easing burdens.

Negative Framing: Calling them "tax breaks for the wealthy" emphasizes inequality and favoritism.

Military Actions:

Positive Framing: Describing military interventions as "peacekeeping missions" suggests a noble and stabilizing effort.

Negative Framing: Referring to military actions as "invasions" or "occupations" highlights aggression and unwelcomed presence.

Bias by Omission

Definition: This occurs when vital information is left out of a story, leading to a biased understanding of the issue.

Example: Omitting key facts that would provide a more balanced view of a controversial topic. The Hunter Biden story is a solid example.

Bias by Placement

Definition: The prominence given to a story can indicate its importance. Placing certain stories on the front page or at the top of a news broadcast can suggest they are more significant.

Example: Giving extensive coverage to a minor scandal while downplaying major policy achievements.

Bias by Spin

Definition: This involves presenting information in a way that subtly persuades the audience to adopt a particular viewpoint.

Example: Using emotionally charged language to describe an event or person. "The Uterus Collector" story by MSNBC cost NBC millions of dollars for a misleading story. [source #24]

Bias by Labeling

Definition: This occurs when certain individuals or groups are labeled in a way that influences public perception.

Example: Referring to a politician as "controversial" or "radical" without providing context.

Bias by Story Selection

Definition: This involves choosing which stories to report based on the outlet's agenda or bias.

Example: Consistently reporting on crimes committed by a specific demographic while ignoring similar crimes by others.

Bias by Source Selection

Definition: This occurs when media outlets choose sources that support their viewpoint while ignoring those that offer an unfamiliar perspective.

Example: Quoting experts who align with the outlet's bias and ignoring those with opposing points-of-view. The erosion of free speech and open debate.

Repercussions are "bounce-backs" from actions or events, intended or unintended. In the aftermath, Democrats scrambled to hide their involvement in concealing the truth about President Joe Biden's mental capacity. Living in denial of the consequences that their actions were unacceptable to the electorate, Democrats failed to grasp the reality that the Donald J. Trump Presidency is a consequence of their actions and inactions.

Democrats were last seen wandering aimlessly in search of integrity, a leader and a platform contributing to the betterment of society. A clear demonstration of the concept - Party before Country.

Was the decision Orwellian when The Democrat Party selected the candidate without an open primary?

Was the Disinformation Governance Board, established on April 27, 2022, at the direction of President Biden and the Democrats, similar to the Ministry of Truth Orwell described?

Down an uncharted path – away from the cliff's edge - for now. We The People, must stay vigilant to political invaders of the People's Republic, DUSA – once-upon-a-time, The United States of America.

Know more than "They" tell you to know.

Knowing is an Advantage!

If "they" concealed facts to protect "their" President, and "The Candidate" - what else did they hide? What facts will they distort as DUSA moves forward? How can we trust deceivers?

Unethical tactics deployed in the fight for power and control, the Biden Administration, the Democrat Party, activist media and partisan loyalists ripped the heart from the "Soul of America" and tarnished their lifelong legacies with deceitful conduct.

In the aftermath, Democrat's visible hatred for Republicans, MAGA and Trump, stems from their totalitarian manipulation of information and suppression of free speech, while concealing the mental acuity of an incumbent President and appointing "The Candidate" - enabling the second term of the Donald J. Trump Presidency.

Why Write This Book?

To interrupt the distortion of facts in a society struggling in a Post-Truth cultural war.

To enlighten people about past accountability and oversight failures. Lessons from our past should not be overlooked.

To stimulate analytical and critical thinking and less drinking of influencer's poison stifling independent thought and open mindedness.

To inspire people to gaze into their own mirror of truth before telling other people what truth is or is not.

Do we need media spin and political propaganda to keep us informed? This is the 21st Century. It's all about tech.

Look around us. Technology companies are partnering to modernize society. Artificial Intelligence is at our fingertips to research and verify information. Learn to use one AI Chatbot to validate the responses from other AIs, media sources, politicians and influencers. Hold them accountable. It's no fun living the consequences of being bamboozled.

Beware of hidden facts and twisted truths.

Excerpt from The United States Declaration of Independence, written by Thomas Jefferson in 1776:

> "We hold these truths to be self-evident, that all men are created equal, that they are endowed by their Creator with certain unalienable Rights, that among these are Life, Liberty and the pursuit of Happiness.--That to secure these rights, Governments are instituted among Men, deriving their just powers from the consent of the governed, --That whenever any Form of Government becomes destructive of these ends, it is the Right of the People to alter or to abolish it, and to institute new Government, laying its foundation on such principles and organizing its powers in such form, as to them shall seem most likely to effect their Safety and Happiness." [source #25]

Awareness is critical in preserving our Rights
to Life, Liberty and the pursuit of Happiness.

Access the sources in this book at **factonpublishing.com**

Notes:

www.ingramcontent.com/pod-product-compliance
Lightning Source LLC
Chambersburg PA
CBHW070818280326
41934CB00012B/3217